the BRIDE'S CHOICE

wedding cakes from South Africa

RIA MEINTJES

EDITED BY: MARGIE SMUTS AND
JACKIE ATHEY

FIRST EDITION/FIRST PRINTING

Continental Publications
PALOS VERDES, CALIFORNIA 90274

DEDICATED TO MAMMA

Continental Publications
PALOS VERDES, CALIFORNIA 90274

"The Bride's Choice"

Copyright 1979 by: Continental Publications

Published in 1979. All rights reserved. No part of the contents of this book may be reproduced in any way without the written consent of the publisher, Continental Publications, 900 Silver Spur Road, Palos Verdes, California 90274.

All rights reserved under Pan American and International Copyright Conventions.

FIRST EDITION

International Standard Book Number: 0-916096-22-X

Library of Congress Catalog Card Number: 79-52243

Manufactured in the United States of America

Acknowledgements: Edited by Jackie Athey; Jacket Design by: Graphics Two; Graphic layout and production by: Graphics Two; Color Separations and printing by: Breene Lithograph.

FOREWORD

I have known Ria Meintjes the last 20 years, since I taught her the very basics of cake decorating. With her happy disposition and her knowledge of baking and decorating, she is one of the cornerstones of the Pretoria branch of the South African Cake Decorators Guild. Her enthusiasm, as well as the knowledge she imparts, is an inspiration to many amateur decorators.

Ria is well known for all kinds of cakes, but her most devoted efforts she puts into designing and decorating wedding cakes. When she decorates a cake for a bride, she puts more into it than mere decoration — she tries to bring out something of the bride's personality and taste; every cake reflects the individual.

This book should prove invaluable not only to prospective brides, who often find it difficult to decide on a wedding cake design, but also to the professional decorator. May this book give pleasure to many a bride and many a decorator.

Margie Smuts.

Margie Smuts

LIST OF ILLUSTRATIONS

LIST OF PATTERNS AND DRAWINGS

CONTENTS

PREFACE

This book was written mainly for South African brides, but since a closer bond between South African and American cake decorators has been established, I have tried to adapt and explain my recipes to also suit Americans. In South Africa, a wedding cake is always a rich fruit cake; however, when it comes to decorating, the same designs usually can be adapted to soft cakes.

The main aim of this publication is to serve as a guide to brides who are looking for something special when ordering their wedding cake. With this work I hope to realize my ambition to furnish the brides of my country (and elsewhere) with ideas for their wedding cakes. I hope, furthermore that this book will provide pleasant reading material as I have not meant it to be a technical manual or a recipe book, but rather a friendly discussion of wedding cakes.

When viewed casually, the cakes may appear to be very similar as so many of them are three-tiered cakes, but when inspected closely each cake offers something different. I have tried to offer such a variety of ideas that the bride will be able to select, say, a flower on one cake, lace work on another, a unique shape in a third, so that eventually she will be able to say, "This is MY cake, not just another cake!"

First and foremost my thanks go to Margie Smuts, my first teacher, who suggested that I write a book like this. Not only has she graciously given permission to use some of her patterns, but many of her ideas are also incorporated in this work.

The photographs were taken by Frikkie and Lenie Dreyer, who were always ready to photograph a cake or two.

The name of our home is "Staan Saam" which means "Stand Together", so to my husband and four sons I can only say that without their unflagging support, I could never have succeeded.

To my Publisher, my deepest appreciation.

The Author

Ria Meintjies

Chapter 1

GENERAL

Cake decorating utensils are rather limited in South Africa, but any person who is genuinely interested can perform near miracles with all kinds of objects around the house and it will not be long before she weighs up every object as to its usefulness in cake decorating. She will view the world through "cake decorating spectacles"! She will discover useful molds, etc. in her kitchen, in the children's toybox and even in the budgerigar's (small parrot) cage for making sugar cradles, bells and a hundred and one beautiful decorations.

When it comes to decorating, the following apparatus, however, is indispensible:

1. A good stout turntable.
2. A rolling pin.
3. A large sharp knife.
4. A surgical palette knife or an exacto knife.
5. Several small water color brushes — numbers 1 to 5.
6. A small pair of tweezers.
7. A pastry wheel.
8. Several marbles — small to large.
9. Various icing tubes (in this book I recommend tubes no's 1, 2, 6, 8, 11, 12, 18, 34).
10. A pair of scissors with a sharp point.
11. Various bottle lids, large and small.
12. Some hors d'oeuvre forks.
13. Some small savory cutters or real petal cutters.
14. Various vegetable colorings.
15. Some waxed paper, greaseproof (Parchment) paper, cellophane and tinfoil.
16. A large mixing bowl, sieve and wooden spoon and/or an electric mixer.

It is important to have a smooth surface to roll out plastic icing or almond paste; table with a panalite top is acceptable. However, for rolling out modeling paste, a plastic covered board, a piece of thick plastic material, or a piece of glass is preferred. A small rolling pin is also essential when modeling flowers; if a small wooden one is not available, a short piece of stainless steel tubing or even a small, round bottle will suffice.

Cake decorating can be a lucrative hobby, but then it must be done on a large scale. Buying small quantities of ingredients at retail shops can be costly, so if you wish to work at a reasonable profit and still produce cakes of good quality, it is essential to buy in bulk. By using only the best ingredients, you can ensure that your customers will be satisfied and that they will tell their friends that your cakes are as good to eat as to look at.

When it comes to using colors, the South African ideal is always to use pastels, except where the natural color of a flower calls for bright colors. Americans evidently like their colors to be bright.

If you are a beginner and you are disappointed with your first efforts, please persevere. Only after constant practice and probably many failures and disappointments, will you feel that you have at last achieved success. When I think back, I can remember how my husband kept saying, "No, my girl, there is no rose that looks like that!" and I, being determined to succeed in making a rose that looks like a rose, kept on practicing until even he had to congratulate me on my beautiful roses.

The best advice that I can give to any beginner is to persevere! It may be a consolation, however, to remember that although you yourself may be aware of many mistakes, usually the bride and her family do not know enough to spot your irregularities. As long as they are satisfied, you can also be satisfied, being determined to cut out your mistakes in the next cake!

Do not over-decorate a cake. Beauty lies in simplicity. Try to have all your ornaments edible. I want to stress this point. I believe that my aversion to artificial ornaments on a wedding cake dates back to my own wedding. There were so many glittering ornaments and artificial flowers on that cake, the cake did not reflect my tastes, and to top it all off, the cake itself was burnt! Now I campaign for cakes that taste as good as they look.

Baking a fruit cake is really not difficult. Gone are the days of coal stoves and guesswork regarding temperature and time, although many a skilled housewife will tell you that for a good fruit cake they would never dream of exchanging their Aga stove, or any other coal range, for an electric oven. However, by setting your temperature correct, the chances of failure with a fruit cake are practically nil.

It has become increasingly popular in South Africa, to use dummy cakes for wedding cakes. By this we mean that the "cake" is actually a wooden or metal model that is decorated, the actual cake being cut up in small pieces and each piece wrapped in cellophane or tin foil and then placed inside the decorated box or model.

Many sleepless nights and working with exact measurements have been my lot in order to meet a bride's requirements. For instance, a lovely young bride told me she wanted her wedding cake to be a model of the "Voortrekker monument". I nearly collapsed! Fortunately, my sons came to my assistance as they looked on the building of such an architectural structure to scale, as a challenge to their ingenuity, and I could give the bride her wish. (See cake No. 28 on page 63) Personally I still favor the traditional wedding cake that does not pretend to be anything other than what it is, but it is always a pleasure to give the bride what she wants, because that is her day, and her cake!

Apparatus needed.

Chapter 2

FRUIT CAKES

In South Africa, no wedding cake, no matter how beautifully it is decorated, is regarded as a proper wedding cake, unless it is also a rich fruit cake. Needless to say, it must also be a delicious cake! As this is essential, I would like to share from my experience some helpful hints regarding the making and baking of fruit cakes. A good basic recipe is needed, to which ingredients may be added or some may be left out, provided the proportion of fruit to the other ingredients remains the same. If the mixture is too soft, the fruit will sink to the bottom and the cake will most probably sink in the center; too much sugar or syrup can also have this effect. A mixture that is too stiff or an oven that is too hot will result in a cake with a point in the center and cracks over the surface. Such a cake will also be very dry.

Prepare the fruit the day before baking the cake. Rub dark and white seedless raisins and currants with a damp cloth as washing the fruit causes a loss of flavor. Of course, if the fruit is really dirty, it will have to be washed, but it should be left to dry thoroughly before mixing. Choice fruit packed in air tight containers, however, is reasonably clean.

Prepare the cake tins by lining them with at least two to three thicknesses of brown paper. Grease each layer well, and use tinfoil for the last layer. When decorating a fruit cake, the cake is always turned over, so the bottom of the cake should be very even. To ensure this, line the sides of the tin first, as follows: Measure the circumference of the cake tin, and cut strips of paper of this length and approximately 10 cm (4 inches) wide. Fold the strips back about 1½ cm (¾ inch) and make slanting cuts along the folded strip. When lining the cake tin, overlap these cuts at the bottom. After all the side pieces have been placed in the cake tin, place the round layers of paper which have been cut to the exact size of the tin, at the bottom. This will ensure a lovely, smooth bottom to the cake.

Care must be taken not to fill the cake tin more than ¾ of its capacity. A fruit cake does not rise very much, so that it will fill the cake tin when baked. Remember also that whereas soft wedding cakes, such as are used in the U.S.A., are made up of several layers for each tier, fruit cakes are comprised of only one layer for each tier. The height of the tier must be in proportion to the diameter of the cake. Bake the cake in a moderate oven 250 degrees Fahrenheit. The time depends on the size of the cake. An average cake of 9 inches in diameter and 4 inches high, will bake from 4 to 5 hours. It sounds funny to say you must "listen" when a cake is done, but it is a very trustworthy method. If you hear a soft buzzing sound when you tap the cake very lightly with your finger in the center, put it back in the oven for at least half an hour as it is definitely not done. Retest after half an hour.

The following recipe for a fruit cake is one that I recommend. It is relatively economical, and if you wish to make it still richer, add more glazed fruit.

Ingredients:
500 grm (1 lb.) butter
500 grm (1 lb.) brown sugar
500 grm (1 lb.) seedless dark raisins
500 grm (1 lb.) seedless white raisins
500 grm (1 lb.) currants
500 grm (1 lb.) chopped dates
250 grm (1/2 lb.) glazed cherries
125 grm (1/4 lb.) candied peel
125 grm (1/4 lb.) chopped or ground
    almonds
125 grm (1/4 lb.) chopped walnuts
8 eggs
2 large tablespoons apricot jam
500 grm (1 lb.) cake flour
1 teaspoon ground ginger
1 teaspoon mixed spice
1 teaspoon ground cinnamon
2 teaspoons baking powder
1 cup sweet wine

Method:
Cream butter and sugar. Add apricot jam. Add eggs, one at a time, beating well each time. Cut dates into small pieces and halve the cherries. Mix all the fruit and dry ingredients well, taking care that the fruit is well covered with flour, as this not only will prevent the fruit from sinking to the bottom but will also ensure an even distribution of the fruit.

This recipe is sufficient for two 9-inch cake tins. When the cake is done, turn it upside down and leave it in the cake tin to cool. Do not remove the paper. When it is taken out of the oven, pour half a cup of sweet wine over it, to keep the cake soft and enhance the flavor. Then seal the cake in plastic. Every week brush a little wine over the cake. This will make the fruit plumper and gives the cake added flavor. The cake must sit for at least one month to six weeks before it is iced.

To ice the cake, use a cake plate (board) which is at least 2 inches (5 cm) larger than the cake. Be very careful when removing the paper from the cake, as some of the fruit may be removed and leave a hole. If such a catastrophe occurs, however, or if a piece of the border is removed, use almond paste to fill in and cover up. Now place the cake (upside down) in the center of the board. Brush more wine over the cake to ensure that the sides are not dry. Now brush a very thin layer of apricot jam over the entire cake. Use the apricot jam sparingly, otherwise the almond paste will slide off. The surface of the cake should only be slightly sticky.

As almond meal is very expensive and rarely obtainable, the simulated almond paste (in packets) is used when necessary. Add a tablespoon of brandy, if difficulty is experienced in rolling the paste out. If the paste is too soft, add a little icing sugar and work in well. The paste must be fairly stiff, not too dry, but also not too soft or it will stick to the rolling pin.

Put a thin layer of icing sugar on the pastry board and roll the paste to a thickness of approximately 1/4 inch (5mm). Lift carefully with both hands and cover the cake with a cloth. Press down on the top of the cake, letting out all air between cake and paste. Now rub down the cake, working from top to bottom to remove all air. The paste must be pressed down onto the cake very firmly, so that it does not break away from the cake when the cake is cut. Also, the almond covering must not become too dry before covering it with icing, as this will make it crumble when cutting the cake. The almond covering must reach to the cake board; cut away any surplus on the board, against the cake. The cake is now ready to be covered with royal or plastic (fondant) icing and to be decorated.

Chapter 3

PLASTIC AND ROYAL ICING

PLASTIC ICING

Now for that miracle, plastic icing! It never becomes very hard, it does not crumble off the cake, and it does not easily turn yellow. One of the ingredients is a preservative, so it can be kept for months and still protect the cake.

Plastic icing is so named because the ingredients are sticky and elastic. I feel that it is the biggest miracle that ever happened in the field of cake icing. Were I a poet, I would write a poem extolling the values of mixing a paste which can be rolled out like a pastry, folded over the cake like a satin cloth, and ready the cake for icing. Gone are the days when the egg whites had to be beaten, icing sugar had to be added by the spoonful, beating after each addition until you were exhausted, and only then did the major job of getting the cake smooth for icing begin. A little icing was spread over the cake, removed, spread over once again and in turn again removed and after hours of effort the result wasn't what you would have liked it to be. And not only one layer, but two or three. Then after a month or two, it had turned yellow!

Ingredients:
2 ounces water
4 ounces liquid glucose
1 ounce gelatine (3 teaspoonfuls gelatine)
2 tablespoons lemon juice plus 1 ounce glycerine
1 drop blue coloring
1 teaspoon flavoring (eg. Rose)
4 - 6 lb. Icing Sugar

Method:
Dissolve the gelatine in cold water and melt over low heat. Cover so that a skin does not form. Add the glucose, which has been slightly heated. Melt together and leave to cool. Add rest of liquid ingredients. NOTE: *INGREDIENTS MUST BE WELL MELTED.*

Make a well in the icing sugar, add liquid and mix to a stiff paste. Do not handle the icing as you would pastry. Press well together and work to a relatively stiff paste, as with putty. It should be used immediately; since it will require re-preparation if it is left for sometime. Remember, no cracks or hard pieces can be tolerated in the icing.

Now brush the cake lightly with the white of an egg. The paste is again rolled out on lightly sprinkled icing sugar and put over the cake. Again, please be very careful that all air bubbles are removed under the plastic icing. Press the plastic icing down very firmly and remove superfluous icing from the board. Your cake is now ready for decorating. It is not necessary to wait for days for the cake to dry prior to decorating.

The next step is to decide on an appropriate border to go around the bottom of the cake in order to seal it securely against dryness and to finish off the cake. Thereafter, any decoration (design) as described in the following chapters can be done on the cake with royal icing. For the borders, a larger star tube, e.g., a number 8 or 12, can be used; for the finer patterns, a number 1 or even 0 or 00 can be used.

ROYAL ICING

The origin of the name royal icing has always puzzled me. In our time, it is not often used in the covering of cakes but it is absolutely essential for the decoration on the cake. One advantage is that it becomes very hard and thus the cake is sealed and protected from air and mites. Also, as royal icing is softer than plastic icing, it can be put through icing tubes and used for making many different border patterns and curls. A small paper-bag with a fine tube through a hole in the front produces beautiful lacework. In earlier days the cake was covered with royal icing, but only a truly experienced person succeeded in obtaining a smooth surface. It also required a second and sometimes even a third covering, which would often turn yellow afterwards.

Although more and more use is made of plastic icing, there are still some people who prefer royal icing. Also, as it is used for decorating the cake; I am including the recipe.

Ingredients:
1 egg white
500 grm (1 lb.) finely sifted icing sugar (Powdered sugar)
Flavoring to taste
1 teaspoon Tartaric acid (or a few drops of acetic acid)
1 teaspoon glycerine

Method:
Beat the egg white stiff, but not dry. Sift in the icing sugar, 1 spoonful at a time, beating well after each addition. It must have the texture of cream and not become clayish. The icing sugar must become completely dissolved in the egg white. The icing has the correct consistency when a peak is maintained after lifting the spoon. For very fine filligree work, leave out the acid and the glycerine and sift the icing sugar through a piece of nylon material. The icing must be beaten if left standing, so that it does not become soggy. Always cover with a slightly wet cloth or stretch plastic to keep out the air.

(Refer to page 54.)

Christelle's Wedding Cake.

15

Chapter 4

DECORATIONS DONE DIRECTLY ONTO THE CAKE

The patterns given as Fig. 3 are all done directly onto the cake. For Fig. 3(a), divide the circumference of the cake into even sections. Now cut a semicircle the size of each division and carefully mark off semicircles along the sides of the cake. Even if you have a lot of experience, this should never be guesswork. With a writer tube (Number 2), lay down a line along the markings, then fill the halfmoon with dots. To make the dots, just rest the point of the tube slightly against the surface of the cake, then stop the pressure before lifting the tube (otherwise a long point will result). Start in the center of the design when making the dots and try to get them evenly spaced.

For Fig. 3(b) the basic work (i.e. drawing the design onto the cake) is the same, only filling in the design is different. Here you use a fine writing tube (1, 0 or 00) and fill the design with cornelli* work. To finish the design, outline the halfmoons with a to-and-fro movement, short and long, using the same fine tube. Cornelli work is very popular, and the design itself can be varied to suit your taste. It gives a very effective finishing touch.
fill the design with cornelli work. To finish the design, outline the halfmoons with a to-and-fro movement, short and long, using the same fine tube. Cornelli work is very popular, and the design itself can be varied

to suit your taste. It gives a very effective finishing touch.

Fig. 3(c) is another variation that goes very well on an oval-shaped cake. It is simply a combination of the first two, with some forget-me-nots added. Notice how the graduated dots finish the outer line.

Fig. 3(d) is used mainly on square cakes. Divide the sides of the cake into even spaces; cut a piece of cardboard to this size and then into a triangle. Mark onto the cake with a pin. Outline the design with straight lines, always working from top to bottom. Fill in the space between the outer lines with cornelli work. With a fine tube make the perpendicular lines in the center. Finish with dots and a small shell border. To make the shells, use a proper shell tube or a star tube. Press the icing so that it forms a blob, stop pressing and pull away the tube along the side of the cake so the icing breaks off. Repeat the action so that the blob just covers the end of the point left when the previous icing broke off.

Fig. 3(e) is very easy and yet very effective, especially for the sides of a round cake. Using a fine writer tube, make a number of small loops around the cake, by simply

---

*Cornelli work is a continuous movement of small curves piped in an irregular pattern almost like a 'crazy path' where it is impossible to find the start and finish.

letting the icing drop from the tube and fixing it to the cake at even points. Now follow up this by "hanging" more loops, to form triangles as shown in the design. It may look complicated, but it is really quite easy when you do it. Finish off with small "fleur-de'lis" decorations also done with the same tube.

LACEWORK DONE ON WAXED PAPER

Lacework entails a lot of work, and is usually done only for show purposes or for a very special person. An experienced deco-rator can use the fine writing tubes, 0 or 00, but the beginner would do well to start off with the thicker writing tubes and a not too intricate pattern.

These lace pieces are made of icing consisting of egg-white and pure icing (powdered) sugar, mixed well. The most important part is sifting the sugar through nylon or silk. Before mixing the icing, stretch a piece of nylon or silk over a plastic container that has a close fitting lid. The sugar, already sifted once through a fine sieve, is now placed, a spoonful at a time, on the nylon, and the lid is placed on the con-tainer, so that the sugar now hangs in a little

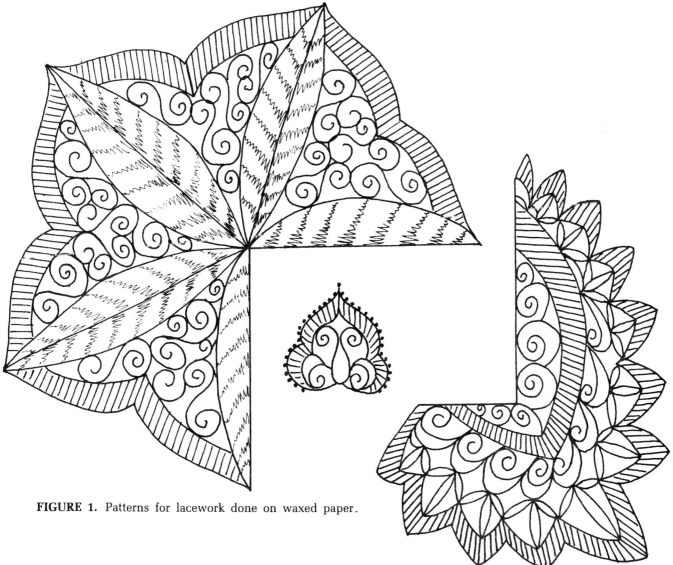

FIGURE 1. Patterns for lacework done on waxed paper.

bag under the lid and inside the container. Now shake the container up and down so that the sugar is sifted through the silk. When removing the lid, take care that the nylon does not slip inside, as the coarser grains of sugar will fall into the container. Place the sifted sugar in a bowl and continue the operation until enough sugar has been sifted.

Beat the egg-white slightly before adding the sifted sugar, then beat the mixture well. If an electric beater is used, the beating must be done very slowly and the mixture allowed to stand so the air bubbles may rise to the top. Sift the sugar just before using to prevent lumps from forming. As one uses very little of this icing at a time and as it is best not to let it stand for days, never mix more than one egg white at a time.

The main secret of making these delicate pieces of lace lies in practice and learning to handle the pieces carefully but with complete confidence. If you require six lace ornaments, make eighteen. You will most probably not break even one in handling

them, because you would not be so nervous, knowing you have enough spares.

Draw the actual size of the pattern you require, on paper. Try to create your own designs. Bear in mind that your design must have enough strong lines to hold it together. Avoid long lines that have little to support them. Study the designs I have given here, and then proceed to design your own pattern. Sometimes I use the pattern in the material of the bride's dress to make my lacework designs.

Now place your pattern on a piece of metal or glass that has been smeared LIGHTLY with margarine or other shortening. Next, smear the pattern very LIGHTLY with margarine, place a piece of wax paper over the pattern (you can even smear this lightly with shortening, but some wax paper is so well waxed that this may not be necessary).

Now do the ornament. When completed, place in a safe place to dry. To remove the lace piece, place the piece of metal for a moment on a hot plate, or if you have

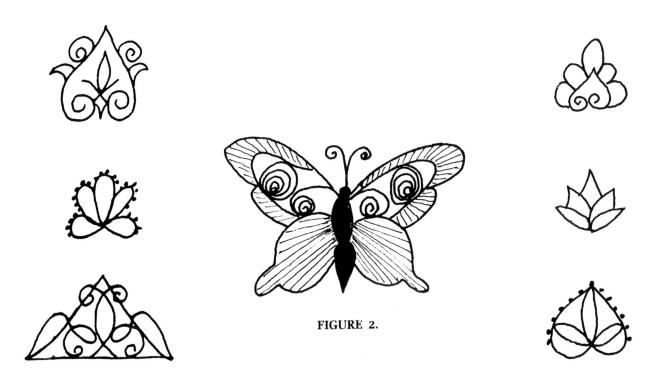

FIGURE 2.

used glass, hold it for a few seconds in a warm oven. Now slip a firm strip of paper under the wax paper, holding the ends of this strip firmly with both hands while you slip it along. Take care not to lift it. The idea is to get the wax paper off the metal or glass. Now slip the wax paper with the ornament into your hand, and carefully pull the wax paper DOWN from under the ornament. Shift the ornament around until it is completely free from the paper.

Be sure to handle the ornament at its strongest point, which, in the case of "wings" is at the point of the 90 degree angle of the base.

LACE POINTS

Small lace points give a wonderful finishing touch to a cake. Try to have a good supply of them on hand as this can often be just what is needed to round off a pattern done on the cake. They are done on wax paper, but it is not necessary to grease the paper as they are small and easily handled.

SUGAR ORNAMENTS

Sugar ornaments are very useful and can replace artificial, bought ones. Any mold can be used as long as you are able to shake out the ornament from it just as a child shakes out a sandcastle from a bucket on the beach.

Mix castor sugar (in the U.S.A., ordinary granulated sugar will do) with egg white to the consistency of wet sea sand. Press this into the mold, for instance, a small plastic bell. When it is full, turn it over and drop the sugar gently out of the bell onto a board. Let it dry for about ten minutes or more if the humidity is high, then lift it very carefully and scrape out the soft sugar inside. A lovely hollow bell will be the result. A sugar "flowerpot" can also be made that way. You need not hollow out the flowerpot as you can fill it with miniature flowers on florist wire, stuck directly into the damp sugar.

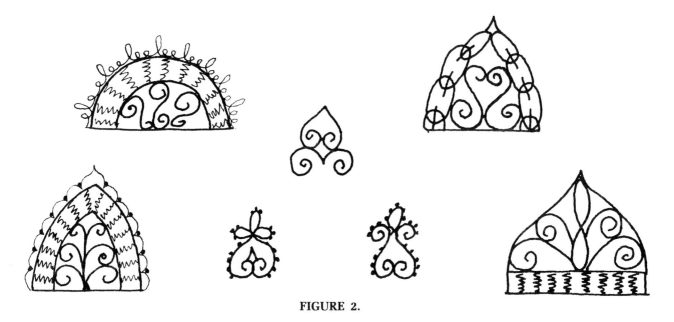

FIGURE 2.

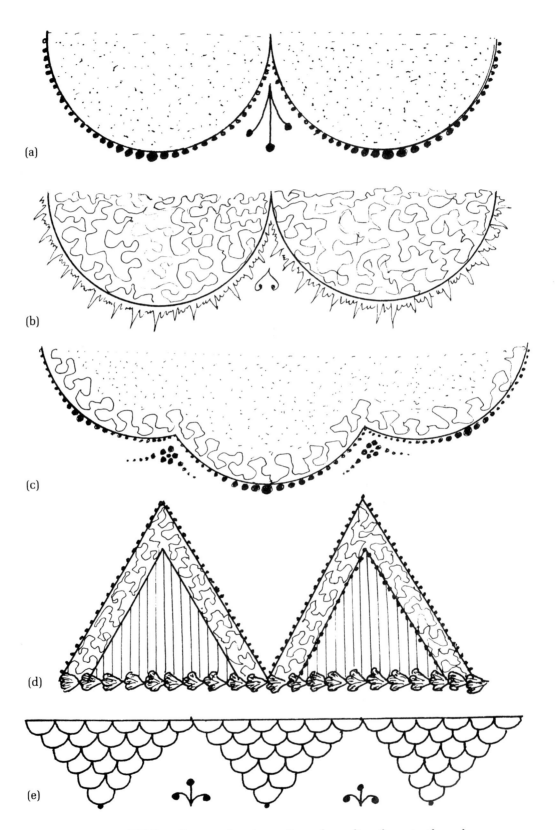

(a)

(b)

(c)

(d)

(e)

FIGURE 3. Patterns for decorations done directly onto the cake.

Chapter 5

FLOW-IN ICING

Flow-in icing is a mixture of egg white and icing (powdered) sugar mixed to a soft consistency so that it flows sluggishly. Ordinary Royal Icing can also be used if water is added to bring it to such a soft consistency. To test whether the icing is the correct consistency, draw a knife across the icing and slowly count to ten. If the sugar has run back evenly so that no mark is visible, by the time you have done that, the consistency is right. If a mark is left after reaching ten, the mixture is too stiff and some more water must be added. If it flows so quickly that there is no mark long before you count to ten, the mixture is too soft and more sugar must be added. The water must be added very gradually to get just the right consistency.

Beautiful effects can be obtained with flow-in icing. Ornaments and figurines can be made in advance to facilitate the finishing off of a cake. All kinds of ideas can be obtained from embroidery transfers, and the lace or the flower patterns of the bride's dress can even be copied.

You can make flow-in motifs separately from the cake, and later attach them to the cake with a little soft royal icing. Draw the design on paper and place it on a level surface — preferably a wooden board or a piece of glass which can be moved if necessary without disturbing the flow-in ornament. Now fix a piece of wax paper over the design, about 10 cm (1 inch) larger than the design. Secure this with cellotape, stretching the wax paper so that it is firm and tight. If the area that is to be flowed-in is large, the wax paper sometimes shrinks before the work is completely dry; therefore, this precaution is essential. Quick drying before a heater will also help to prevent shrinkage.

Start the design by piping the outline in royal icing. If the design calls for different colors, be sure to pipe the different outlines in the appropriate colors. Allow the piping to dry; a crust should form before going any further. The experienced decorator will be able to fill the outline in the pattern without disturbing the outline, even if it is not quite dry, but the beginner should not attempt this too soon.

Fig. 4. A flow-in flower motif that can be used very effectively on the sides of a large cake. I suggest that you do it in the same color as the cake itself, or to use various shades of the same color. Using a fine writer tube and royal icing, pipe the outline of the flower. Where one petal joins the other, carry on with only one line. Now, while the outlines are drying, dilute the icing to the right flow-in consistency; be careful while doing this not to beat in air bubbles. Put this soft icing in a paper bag, taking care not to fill it to the top, and carefully close the top of the bag by folding it securely several times. Now turn the bag so that the point shows to the top, carefully cut away the point, turn the bag down and slowly let the icing flow into the appropriate part of the pattern. Fill one division at a time, and wait until it is relatively dry before filling the adjacent division, otherwise the icing will simply flow from the one to the other.

Fig. 5. A loose lid or collar on top of the cake can be very effective. If the cake is covered in a light pastel color and the collar is done in colors that tone in, it can be very pleasing. Remember the rule: no two thin lines next to one another, and no two adjoining divisions to be filled one after the other.

Leave the collar for at least a day to dry properly. Should the humidity be very high, a heater or lamp may be placed nearby to dry out the air. When the collar is dry, carefully turn it over and remove the paper.

FIGURE 4. Flow-in flower motif.

Turn it over again, and handle it only at the strongest points. Now place a paper drawing of the design on the cake, and prick a hole through the paper where there is a large flow-in section. Remove the paper and with royal icing secure a sugarcube to act as a pillar where the marks are on the cake. Pipe a little royal icing also on top of the pillar and carefully place the collar onto the pillars. The flow-in collar is thus raised above the cake, giving the impression of depth.

Fine trellis work or lace points can be used to finish off edges of the collar, giving the impression that the collar is actually "resting" on the points. When dry it can also be shaded using a fine paint brush.

Flow-in icing can also be used to make swans and other ornaments that are used on wedding cakes. One often finds that a flow-in heart or bell is just the thing to fill in an open space.

FIGURE 5. Template for a collar or lid. (a quarter of actual template).

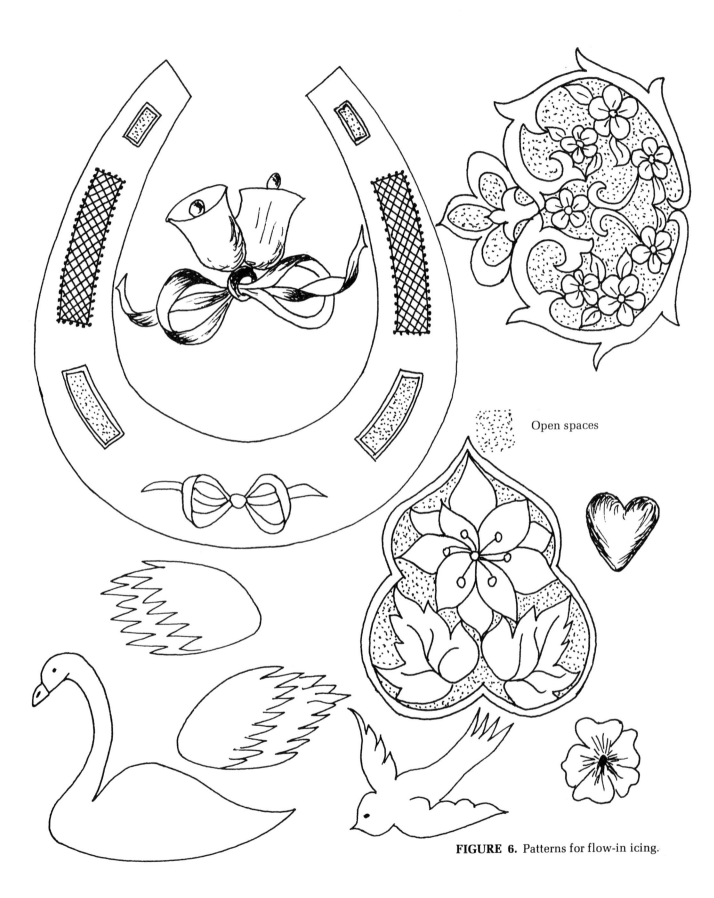

Open spaces

FIGURE 6. Patterns for flow-in icing.

Chapter 6

HAND MODELLING

With good modelling paste, or clay as it is sometimes called, you can copy flowers from nature. Remove the petals from a real flower and draw the outline on paper. You can now use this to cut out your petals once they are rolled out, or you can fashion a cutter from soft tin; a good set of cutters for the different kind of flowers facilitates matters. In South Africa it is now possible to have cutters made to order through the Cake Decorator's Guild. In the U.S.A. you can order through Continental Publications or your favorite cake decorating supply shop.

RECIPE FOR MODELLING CLAY.

Ingredients:
Approximately 2 cups icing
   (powdered) sugar
2 teaspoons Gum Tragacanth
3 teaspoons gelatine
2 teaspoons cold water
1 teaspoon liquid glucose
1 egg white. (Do not use frozen egg
   white)

Method:
Heat 1 cup icing sugar and gum powder in the top of a double boiler. Mix well to prevent the gum from forming lumps. Soak the gelatine in cold water and allow to melt very slowly. Add the teaspoon of glucose as soon as the gelatine is melted. As soon as the icing sugar and gum are warm and the gelatine melted and the glucose mixed with it, mix everything together, including the egg white, which should be at room temperature. Add the remaining icing sugar and mix to a stiff paste. Knead well. Cover well in stretch plastic so that all air is excluded and leave overnight. Before using, knead well again. If it is too stiff, a little vegetable shortening may be kneaded in. It also helps to smear your hands with shortening when kneading the clay. It can now be divided into smaller portions and colored with vegetable coloring.

A special board is necessary for rolling out this clay. I recommend the following: stretch a piece of smooth plastic material over a pastry board and grease the surface lightly with margarine or vegetable shortening. Use a small rolling pin, or even a round medicine bottle.

1. ROSES.

Although they are not the easiest of flowers to make, roses are one of the most popular flowers; any decorator should learn to make a good rose. Basically all rose petals are the same shape. They are made bigger or smaller according to the size of the flower required.

Start with a piece of modelling clay about the size of an ordinary marble. Knead it well. It is important that you knead each piece of clay that you use, very well. Press it down firmly onto the plastic-covered board and shape it like a fan. Now roll it out holding the roller at a slant so that the edges become paper thin. The center of the fan will be thicker as this will form the centerpiece of your rosebud. If you are using rose petal cutters, you will still roll out your petal to get the edges paper thin. The first petal is rolled up completely to form the inner cone of the rosebud. The second petal is made similarly and then placed over the first as if

Full-blown rose and the cutters used for the petals.

you were giving it a cap or wrapping a baby in a blanket. Press firmly at the bottom and shape the top of the petal by curling it slightly backwards. Continue in this way, each time curling the petal slightly. Place a real rose in front of you and notice how the petals are curled. The petals are not made bigger as your rose grows bigger, only more and more petals are added in a circular movement. Cut away superfluous sugar from the bottom every now and then. Use a little egg white to stick the petals on if they do not adhere by themselves.

Rose leaves: Color a piece of modelling clay green. To obtain the natural green of a rose leaf, add a drop of black coloring, but be very careful not to use too much — try for just a suggestion of black. Press the piece of clay flat, then add a few drops of yellow, green and brown directly onto the clay. Use a sharp knife and "cut" the colorings into the paste. Just press it together again but do not knead — the colors must not mix. Now use a small piece at a time and roll it out onto the greased surface. To give the leaf a natural appearance, use a real leaf with prominent veins to press onto the clay and cut it out with a sharp palette knife, or use a leaf cutter. Using the thumb and forefinger of each hand, pick up the leaf, bend it slightly and place it somewhere to dry. The spots and stripes of the concentrated coloring gives it the appearance of having collected some dust, and also gives the effect of light and shadow. These flowers and leaves get quite hard and can be kept a long time.

2. AN OPEN ROSE

This must not be confused with a dog-rose. It is simply a rose that is more open than a bud. It can consist of more than one row of petals. Color the modelling clay the desired color. The inside petals can be slightly darker than the outside ones. Notice on plate No. 2 how the cutters vary from small to large. Thinly roll out a knob of clay and cut out a few petals. Roll the edges of the petal paper thin. Shape the petal by placing it in a rounded utensil or over a large marble. Curl the edges backwards. Leave to dry. Make a number of petals in this way, using a smaller bowl or marble for cupping the smaller petals. Should a large rose be required, make a set of even larger petals. To assemble the rose, place a piece of wax paper in the bottom of a lid, wax side uppermost. Pipe some royal icing sugar on the paper and arrange the petals to overlap one another. Start with the outer layer of petals; five are usually enough. The petals of the second layer should be so arranged that the petals of the second layer overlap those of the first layer. See plate No. 2. Now pipe a blob of yellow royal icing in the center and add a few stamens. When the flower has dried completely, you can draw some veins on the petals using a very tiny brush. Even the edges of the petals could receive a hint of color in a slightly darker shade.

A bouquet of flowers.

Arum Lilies and Proteas.

3. THE ARUM LILY (CALLA LILY)

Use some ice cream cones over which to dry the petals. The basic idea is the same as for the rose: first shape the petals and let them dry before assembling the flower. Study a lily to get the shape of the petal or use a cutter. The petals are thin around the edge, but thick at the bottom, and more in the shape of a triangle than are the rose petals. Shape the petal over the cone to dry.

The petal will be hanging upside down over the cone. Lift the sides of the petal with a paint brush and pinch the tip to a point; bend slightly back. Leave to dry. To make the pistils, roll a small piece of bright yellow clay into the shape of the pistil, thick at the base and with a blunt point at the top. While the pistil is still soft, roll it in sugar to form pollen. Leave to dry. When both pieces are dry, put them together with a little royal icing.

A Cake decorated with Frangipani.

4. FRANGIPANI.

This flower is very popular in South Africa for bridal bouquets, and, therefore, also for their wedding cakes. This is not the easiest flower to make, although it looks easy, so do not be discouraged if your first attempt fails.

Cut five petals. If you do not happen to have the correct cutter, use the medium size rose petal cutter and cut the sides away a little. The paste must not be rolled too thin in this case as it is a wax-like flower with thickish petals. Slightly curl the left side of each petal. Shape the flower over an ice cream cone, letting the petals overlap one another. Dampen them slightly with egg white to let them stick to one another. Use cotton or tissue paper to fan the petals slightly outwards. Let it dry. The frangipani does not have stamens. Paint the inside of the flower light yellow at the bottom, letting the color fade away towards the top. On the outside, a little yellow paint can be stroked around the very bottom also letting it fade away.

To form the bud, roll a piece of clay in an oblong shape, thick at the bottom and forming a blunt point at the top. With a knife make five grooves lengthwise and twist it clockwise to give the appearance of folded petals. A covered piece of florist wire can be stuck into the lower end. When dry, touch the supposed edges of the petals lightly with very, very pale pink.

5. THE DAISY OR MARGUERITE.

This can easily be made by using an appropriate cutter, or else the petals could be cut out separately and left in a shallow bowl or over curved shapes to dry. When dry, put them together in a shallow lid on a piece of wax paper, using royal icing to hold them in shape. Pipe a blob of yellow royal icing in the center and drop some yellow nonpareils on the soft icing for pollened stamens, or form the stamens by piping small yellow dots with a fine writer tube.

6. THE ORCHID.

This is the prize flower for any bride. There are many different kinds of orchids, with the most popular one being the cataleaya orchid. This is the one that I am going to describe. The color combinations of this orchid lends itself marvelously for bridal cakes, as one can then easily introduce the color scheme of the wedding. For instance, so often when a bride has blue as her color scheme, it poses a problem for the cake decorator, but by using a cataleaya orchid this can be overcome if you paint the inside of

Marguerites.

31

Frangipani, Marguerite, rose and orchid.

the trumpet blue and tinge the edges of the petals with blue.

Cutters for the cataleaya orchid are fairly easily obtainable; or, you can cut a pattern on paper and cut out your petals from that. For drying the petals use apple holders. Patty pans are also very useful. The trumpet can be dried over an ice cream cone or metal cream horn cone. The three long petals with grooves drawn down the length are put down in a triangle as shown on plate No. 4. Bend them slightly for the natural look. The three other petals call for more proficiency. Flute the edges of the two side petals using a wooden tool or the back part of a No. 5 paintbrush. Do the fluting slant-wise. Draw a line down the center of the petal. As you do the fluting, keep lifting the thin part every now and then to help it along. The petal now has a crinkle-cut, ser-rated edge.

Leave them to dry over a curved sur-face. The trumpet is cut out and fluted in the same way and dried over a cone. Cut a groove from the back so that royal icing can be piped through on assembling. Now pre-pare the pistil. Study a real orchid (or a good picture) to see the shape; it is elongated with a slightly flat tip. Assemble the flower, using royal icing to attach the different pet-als, according to the picture shown. Sup-port the petals with cotton or tissue until dry. Color the trumpet the desired color before putting in the pistil.

The Giant Protea.

7. THE PROTEA.

Start by shaping the inner part from modeling clay. It is cone-shaped and pink in color. Cover this with long stamens completely, using the finest writer tube; the stamens come to a point at the top. The stamens also have to be pink in color, slightly softer in color than the petals. The petals are made separately. First, cut out the outer petals using an oblong petal cutter; the petal must have a sharp point. Let them dry over a rounded surface. Placing them inside a bowl ensures they all will have the same amount of curvature. Do the same with the second row of petals. When dry, attach them to the finished cone, using royal icing. Be careful in handling the flower as the petals are thin and the cone is heavy. When dry, paint the points and the inside of the petals a darker shade of pink. Now sprinkle a little edible silver powder over the protea, and all the trouble has been worthwhile!

Of course, this is the giant protea, which is the national flower of South Africa. There are many other kinds of protea, but it would take a whole book to describe each one of them, so this one will suffice.

Cake with bouquet of Anthiriums.

8. THE ANTHIRIUM.

This flower is also very popular as a bridal bouquet, and, therefore, also on the bridal cake. It looks very easy to make, but do not be fooled. It looks very much like the arum lily, but it needs quite some experience to model a successful anthirium. Giving significance to those veins and curves requires skill. Roll the clay so that when you have cut out the flower, the edges are very thin. Press it into a shallow, hollow receptacle to dry. Remember to make a groove on the back of the petal and pinch the point of the petal with thumb and forefinger. To make the pistil, use a piece of florist wire, and mold the pistil around it, and give it the correct shape. When the pistil is dry, dip it in egg white, then roll it in yellow castor sugar. Now you have the petals and the pistils, but the petals are dull whereas the anthirium has shiny waxy petals. Even painting them with edible lacquer, leaves the petals dull. Only after many tries did I find the solution: heat a relatively strong sugar solution and "wash" the flowers in it. This alone gives a lovely shine like the real anthiriums!

Try to copy any flower in the garden. With practice and patience you can do it and experience the joy of creating something in sugar that looks like the real thing. Sugar is so acccommodating and elastic, when made up into our modelling paste, that you can copy every fold and every groove of the real flower with practice and patience. During those months when there are not so many weddings that I have the time to model, I fill boxes full of different flowers and leaves so that when a wedding cake is commissioned at short notice, it can easily be done.

Chapter 7

WEDDING CAKES — ONE- TWO- AND THREE-TIERED.

GENERAL HINTS FOR WEDDING CAKES.

When deciding on the type of wedding cake, the bride's own taste, the size of the reception, the overall color scheme, and even her personality, must be taken into consideration. For a happy-go-lucky tomboy, for instance, you would choose a cake much different from one for the more sedate and sober bride. The type of cake must match the bride! It is not always so easy to offer something different to every bride, but sometimes it is just the choice of flower, or a different accent in color that makes a cake different from the others. You have to take time to decide, together with the bride (and her mother), and when you make a suggestion be prepared to have it rejected; then start all over again until she is satisfied. After all, it is HER big day!

A very important factor that must come into consideration is the size of the reception. Once that has been established, you can really start planning in earnest. For a small intimate reception, a one-tier cake should suffice, but if they anticipate about 300 guests, at least a three-tiered cake would be needed. Also, the bride should decide whether she wants any of the cakes to be dummies. Furthermore, she has to decide whether she would like the bottom tier to be a hollow dummy into which the wrapped pieces of cake will be packed, or a solid cake to be cut at the reception.

Brides are as unpredictable as the weather! Also, if they have set their minds on something specific, they very seldom will listen to advice. I remember the time when a bride came to me with the request for a five-tiered cake. On further questioning it came to light that there was going to be a very small family gathering, and no big reception! I pointed out to her that such a cake would be out of place and that it was the sort of cake that one would have at a very big reception in a large hall, but she was not to be moved — she wanted a five-tiered cake — and she got it! By the way, I should warn you that special care has to be taken when you have so many tiers, especially if all the tiers are real cakes.

A fruit cake is relatively solid, but with a weight of approximately 50 kilograms resting on it, you have to reinforce it. It is then best to use pillars with skewers going right down into the cake. If you do not have them, you can put foil-covered sticks inside the cake at the point of gravity.

Cakes of different shapes call for cake-boards of the same shape, but at least 2 inches bigger all around than the cake itself. Do not over decorate the cake. A very neat, well finished cake is much more attractive than an over decorated cake. The beauty of the cake is very often in the simplicity of the decoration.

To a person leafing through this book, it may seem that the cakes do not really differ very much from one another, but when analyzing them you will find them all different. Superficially, to me the paintings of a great artist, like our Pierneef, may all look very similar, but to the person who knows more about it than I do, there will be a world of difference in them.

I do not make use of artificial ornaments — I only use flowers and ornaments made from sugar. The designs of the cakes are all original and my own.

ONE AND TWO-TIERED WEDDING CAKES.

No. 1. One-tiered square wedding cake.

NO. 1. SQUARE ONE-TIERED CAKE.

A cake of only one tier is far more appropriate for a small intimate wedding than a large, many tiered cake. For an informal family gathering this cake is ideal. A square cake is easy to cut, and there is no waste. Cutting the cake at the reception always creates a friendly atmosphere.

For the decoration of this cake, two small horseshoes and two swans are made in advance in flow-in icing (see chapter 5), also the orchids, arum lilies and marguerites on the corners are made in advance. When using orchids, you should not use too many other flowers, as they are a decoration on their own. Fine linework, reminiscent of the fine bridal array, is done on top of the cake, and tiny flow-in hearts form the lower border.

No. 2. Oval One-tiered Wedding Cake.

NO. 2. OVAL ONE-TIERED WEDDING CAKE.

As the shape of this cake is oval, it is different from the usual; I have found it to be an immediate favorite with brides.

The whole cake is covered in diagonal block trellis work. The pattern of the trellis work on the sides is shown in Fig. 3(e) in Chapter 4. Done in white over a very pale pink coating, it has the appearance of a misty veil drawn over the cake. (In South Africa, we never use harsh colors — always very pale, pastel colors.) The bottom border consists of leaves made from molding paste. A bouquet of orchids, arum lilies and other small flowers completes the cake.

No. 3 Square One-Tiered Wedding Cake.

NO. 3. SQUARE ONE-TIERED WEDDING CAKE.

I include this cake mainly because of a discovery that I made when doing it, that may help someone else. The first time I made this cake, I did not have a roller with a pattern on it, and I had this idea of covering the cake in a block pattern. I was standing in my kitchen wondering how to do it, when I saw an old rusted screw lying on the window sill. I took the screw and started rolling it onto a piece of modeling clay that I had in my hand . . . and there in front of my eyes was the most perfect set of lines that the grooves had made! I was as excited about this discovery as Archimedes must have been when he jumped out of his bath! I started to experiment, and these perfectly neat blocks were the result! Incidently, I also use this idea when making the markings of the pages of a book. Maybe this "dis-

No. 4. Square Two-tiered Cake.

covery" of mine will come in handy to someone who does not possess a roller with markings on it.

The bottom border is done with a large star tube by pushing out a blob and pulling it upwards against the side of the cake, and then overpiped with a writer tube. The dots are done with a writer tube, and the whole is finished off with a bouquet of flowers.

NO. 4. SQUARE TWO-TIERED CAKE.

Daisies and trellis done directly onto the cake make a pleasing wedding cake. In this case, the trellis lines have been overpiped carefully to build them up. They can be overpiped three or four times, but care must be taken that each layer is perfectly dry before the next is piped over. When done well, this gives the effect of a honeycomb. Using a rose-leaf tube (No. 11), a frill is piped around the outer edge of the trellis work. The lower border is similar to that of cake No. 3, and is done with a star tube. Pipe a thin line along the top of the up-right shells and you have the effect of balle-rinas joining hands. Arrange the flowers on tulle to soften and enhance the overall effect. The tulle also serves to give a good focal point and allows the flowers to be placed on various depths. the flowers may also be wired to allow for this effect.

No. 5. Oval Two-Tiered Wedding Cake.

NO. 5.   OVAL TWO-TIER WEDDING CAKE.

This is another oval creation that proved very popular because of its unusual shape. The candle on top is optional, but it helps to accentuate the shape. Candles on cakes are modern and popular. The color of the cake is a matter of taste, and the color of the flowers are chosen to complement or accentuate the basic color of the cake. Open roses in apricot and orchids in mauve are the main decorations. For a gay, colorful effect, small, white ribbon bows have been used.

No. 6. Heart-shaped Two-tiered Wedding Cake.

NO. 6.   HEART-SHAPED TWO-TIER WEDDING CAKE.

Love is the basis for any wedding and the heart is regarded as the seat of love, so a heart-shaped wedding cake seems most appropriate. The two tiers are separated with a tripod stand. Two bouquets of yellow roses are the main decorations, while the sides are decorated with hearts.

No. 7. Two-Hearts Wedding Cake.

THREE-TIERED WEDDING CAKES.

NO. 7.   TWO-HEARTS WEDDING CAKE.

On each of the two cakes I have placed a bouquet of frangipani. Arrange the two cakes so that it will appear as if the two points flow one into the other. The heart effect is repeated around the cake. Use dots to fill the hearts. Filigree piping on the top of the cakes and a star border finishes off the whole.

NO. 8.   THREE-TIERED CAKE WITH PROTEAS (A)

Different effects can be obtained by the arrangement of the cakes. Square cakes can be placed directly above one another or they may be placed so that the corners do not correspond. In this case I made use of a single chrome pillar in the center and placed the cakes squarely on top of each other. Line-work on the sides is really the only decora-

No. 8. Square Three-tiered Wedding cake with Proteas (A).

tion apart from the border, so that the flowers can really show up. Proteas are heavy flowers, but as it is our national flower, and a bride asks for it, one has to try and soften the whole effect by also making use of smaller flowers in between.

No. 9.   Three-tiered Wedding cake with Proteas (B).

NO. 9.   THREE-TIERED WEDDING CAKE WITH PROTEAS (B)

These cakes are the same size, but arranged differently. I had the chrome stand made specially for this cake. Note the interesting way in which the cakes are placed. The back points of the lower cakes meet behind the third cake, to form a triangle.

Although the color of the giant protea is actually light pink, here I used "poetic license", since the bride wanted them to match her color scheme. They were done in a very pale yellow. A little linework on the sides was all that was needed to effectively finish off these cakes. For a large reception one can even place another smaller cake on top of the center one.

No. 10.   Three-tiered Square Wedding Cake with Orchids.

NO. 10.   THREE-TIERED SQUARE WEDDING CAKE WITH ORCHIDS.

Here the tiers are again placed in a different way, making this cake something special in the placing of the cakes. I very thinly rolled out the icing for the "handkerchiefs" draped over the corners, and finished them off with tiny dots. The stems of the flowers are gathered in a bow and arranged so that the bouquet on one tier does not obscure that on the next tier.

The popular idea in South Africa is not to have a tall top ornament on the cake nor to use artificial decorations on the cake, so the arrangement on the top cake is just another bouquet, lifted in the center with a ribbon.

A cake like this requires hours of hard work, but when the bemused, bright-eyed bride goes into ecstasies about it, you feel that all your hours of toil have been worthwhile!

No. 11. Round Three-Tiered Wedding Cake.

NO. 11. ROUND THREE-TIERED WEDDING CAKE.

Although this is the traditional round wedding cake, I have again broken away from the usual pillars by using a central chrome pillar. However, this cake could just as well have been done using four pillars under each tier. The flowers would then just have been arranged differently.

The linework on the cakes are very simple, and the border was done with a star tube for the upright shells and a fine writer tube for the stringwork. When using molded flowers, the rest of the decoration should be kept as simple as possible.

Where the arrangement of the flowers are done around the pillar, as in this case, the cake looks the same from any angle and can very effectively be displayed in the center of a hall.

No. 12.   Round Three-tiered Wedding Cake with Marguerites.

NO. 12.   ROUND THREE-TIERED WEDDING CAKE WITH MARGUERITES.

In this cake the accent falls mainly on the flowers. The sides of the cake are finished off with line and stringwork, while the border is done in an interesting way.

With a small star tube, I made a plaited border and then placed a star flower in each hollow. These flowers are very easy to make. Simply cut them with a star cutter, which can be found in any set of savoury cutters, and then place them over a marble to dry so that there is a slight curve to the petals. The centers, as in the case of the marguerites, are done with a small writer tube.

No. 13. Three-Tiered Horseshoe Cake.

NO. 13.   THE HORSESHOE WEDDING CAKE.

This is not an easy cake to do, but it is very popular with brides. Care must be taken with the decoration on the sides as the pattern may well change as the curvature of the cake changes. Therefore, it is best to use a decoration that can be adapted, i.e. prefer-ably one that is not connected. The decoration should be kept simple as the shape of the cake as well as the flower arrangements already makes it something special.

The horseshoe on the top and the swans are done in flow-in icing, and the flowers are arranged so that they flow out of the horseshoe. Orchids, arum lilies and smaller flowers were used.

No. 14.   Round Balls Wedding Cake (A).

NO. 14.   ROUND BALLS WEDDING CAKE (A)

For a while it was the fashion to have the wedding bouquets in the form of a ball. The ball was formed with net and the flowers were stuck into it. Sometimes feathers were also used like this. When a bride, however, came to me one day and requested her cake also to be in this shape, I needed to do some thinking. By using two bowls, equal in size, the cake was baked, and then placed together to form a ball. For more than a year after that first cake, the balls reigned supreme as the most sought after wedding cake! I had to have chrome pillars specially made to support the cakes, but it was worthwhile.

The success of this cake is that everything must be round . . . no front or back . . . the same all around! The decoration must be simple and the flowers not too big.

No. 15. Round Balls Wedding Cake (B).

NO. 15.   ROUND BALLS WEDDING CAKE (B)

In this instance, the cakes were placed one on top of the other, with a broomstick going right through them, and placed on a tripod stand.

The cakes themselves are covered with stars (my erstwhile teacher, Margie Smuts always maintained that stars were the sign of an amateur who did not know how to use her tubes properly, but in this instance the stars really proved very effective).

The orchids were arranged to resemble a waterfall, and covered florist wire helped to give the correct curved line to the arrangement.

No. 16.   Oval Three-Tiered Wedding Cake with
Anthiriums.

NO. 16.   OVAL THREE-TIERED WEDDING CAKE WITH ANTHIRIUMS.

As described in Chapter 6, the anthirium is a flower akin to the arum lily and yet very different. Anthiriums and birds done in flow-in icing are the main decoration of this cake. The flowers are arranged so that a good balance in the cake itself is obtained.

A diamond linework pattern done with a small writer tube on the sides and the border done with a small star tube in a zig-zag movement completes the decoration.

No. 17. A Study In Yellow.

NO. 17.   A STUDY IN YELLOW.

Here the accent falls on the flowers. The flowers, even the small ones, were all wired so as to simplify the making of the bouquets. Also, much attention was given to the shading of the flowers, the larger flowers being lighter than the smaller ones.

The sides were done in the Pattern 3(d) given in Chapter 4. The lower border was done as follows. First, upright shells were done with a large star tube. Then stringwork was done connecting the points, and then more strings were done connecting points in between the shells. A narrow ribbon was fixed onto the cake with icing, just above the star points. The stringwork was continued over the ribbon.

No. 18. Three-tiered Waterfall Wedding Cake.

NO. 18. THREE-TIERED WATERFALL WEDDING CAKE.

This cake was made to represent a waterfall by arranging the flowers so they cascade in a mass from the top of each cake down to the board. This is repeated in each cake. Care must be taken, however, to maintain a good balance in the cake as a whole. The lower border of each cake is a row of flow-in hearts. The sides of the cake may be left bare, but in this case the choice of the bride was a flow-in motif to resemble guipure lace.

Chapter 8

NOVELTY WEDDING CAKES

Almost without exception there are sentimental memories attached to these cakes, so please bear with me as I share them with you.

NO. 19. CHRISTELLE'S WEDDING CAKE.

This was the cake I made for my petite daughter-in-law, the bride of my eldest son. On this cake I used almost every kind of icing technique. The idea was that the cake should symbolize the coming together of two persons in matrimony to become a single entity.

The cakes and the top flow-in motif were "framed" in fine filigree motifs done with a 00 tube. This is nerve wrecking but very rewarding, and the kind of work that one only does for love — never for payment as no money can compensate you for the hours of labor and the strain on the nerves. When making lacework like this, however, it is wise always to make three times the number of motifs that you would need, because the psychological effect on you then is that you handle the motifs with confidence because you are not afraid of them breaking, and consequently you do not break them.

In the center of this cake I made a spiral shaped holder, in which the small bouquet

No. 19. Christelle's Wedding Cake.
(A detailed photo on page 15.)

was arranged. This was also supposed to be symbolical indicating the years leading to a fuller and richer life.

NO. 20. THE OX WAGON.

When brides came to me with unusual requests for their cakes, it was usually my eldest son, who is an engineer, who came to my rescue in constructing the models for me to cover and decorate. These "cakes" were usually dummies that had the actual pieces of cake wrapped up in tinfoil inside. This is often done in South Africa, where the traditional wedding cake is always a rich fruit cake. When the eldest son got married and left home, the second son, who was then studying to be a land surveyor, took over, and this cake was his first "consignment". This specific bride had her whole wedding centered around the ox wagon. The cake was to be symbolic of the couple starting out on the unknown road. Ox wagons are not so plentiful today, that one can just sit down and make one. A careful study had to be made, and, fortunately, Pretoria being such an historical city, there were quite a few wagons that could be studied in the different museums.

When the bride arrived at the church also in an ox wagon, the cake really did not look out of place.

No. 20. The Ox Wagon.

No. 21. The Boat of Love.

NO. 21.   A BOAT OF LOVE.

This bride, a medical practitioner, was very definite about what her wedding cake should look like, and she and I spent hours planning it. The name of the boat was "Amour" — "love".

Instead of cutting the "cake" which again was a dummy iced over, the anchor rope was cut symbolizing the boat setting off on its voyage. In this case, the moment the rope was cut a light went on behind the sails. The sails were made of modeling paste cut according to a pattern and curved over different round objects.

No. 22. The Bell.

NO. 22.   THE BELL.

Again, the bell itself is only an iced-over dummy. To give the impression that the bell was hanging, it was placed on a central pillar so that it was lifted well above the table. This was placed on a small round table, and from under the bell, the wrapped pieces of cake "fell" right almost to the floor and obscured the pillar. It was most impressive. Each of the 500 pieces were tied with yellow and white ribbon. I have also used the bell placed slantwise, with the cake falling out of it.

It does not, however have to be a dummy cake. I have already done it in a solid cake, and I have even done a three-tiered bell cake in solid cake. In that case, the central pillar that supports them is camouflaged to give the appearance of being the handle of the bell.

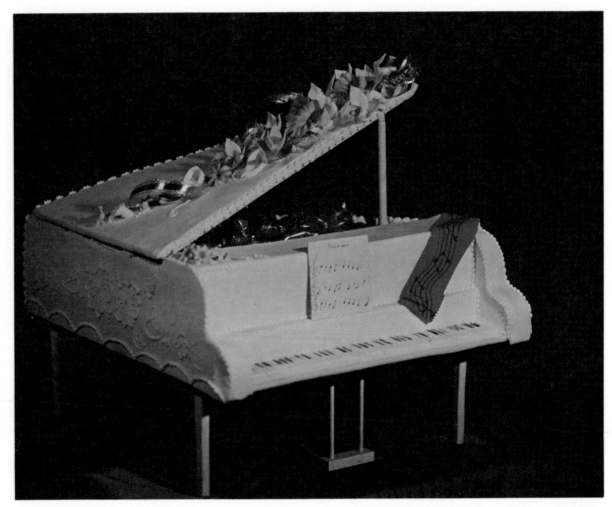

NO. 23.   THE PIANO.

For a musical couple, this design is very popular. Sometimes the pieces of cake are packed inside the piano and the lid lifted when the "cake" is "cut". One bridegroom had a very original idea. He asked for a tape recording of the wedding march to be placed inside the piano (of course the whole tape recorder had to go inside), so when they "cut the cake" the music started. The dummy was made of wood; therefore, it can be made to any size. It is very necessary to give attention to all the fine details, otherwise it may not really look like a piano. However, it is also possible to make this in a solid cake by baking two cakes and cutting them into the appropriate shapes, but that will not suffice for a large gathering.

No. 24. The Horn of Plenty.

NO. 24. THE HORN OF PLENTY.

It is sometimes said that the wedding cake is the symbol of "abundance" because every couple hope and pray for abundance of love and good fortune. As such then, this cake is very appropriate.

Making this dummy can be very tedious. The base of the horn was made of wire gauze bent into the desired shape. A layer of cotton was then placed over it and covered with plastic material to make it firm. The front portion was cut out of cardboard and attached to the wire. An opening was left through which the cake could be taken. Only then was the cake covered with plastic icing.

The whole was plaited like a basket using a small star tube. What a major operation that was! Anyone who has done canework knows how to "steal" a line, and that is also how you do this plaiting where the point of the cornucopia is small; it becomes reasonably big at the opening. An arrangement of flowers finishes the whole.

No. 25. The Champagne Glass.

NO. 25.   THE CHAMPAGNE GLASS.

This "cake" is sometimes used as the wedding cake itself, and sometimes it is used in conjunction with another cake, holding the wrapped pieces of cake. The base is decorated with modelled flowers, and a small posie, of modelled flowers is also placed on top of the pieces of cake.

No. 26, The Wine Barrel.

NO. 26. THE WINE BARREL.

With the modern trend of wine and cheese receptions, this cake has become very popular. Of course, this can be a solid cake, but with our wrapped pieces of cake, it is easier to make a dummy, cover it with plastic icing and decorate it to look like a wine cask. Making the grapes is rather a tedious business, but worthwhile in the end. Each grape has to be made separately, and the best way to make them is to stick a wire with a hook into each ball and to hang them up to dry, else they will have a flat side to them. When perfectly dry and firm, they can be painted. Only then do you gather them into bunches. To make the leaves, try pressing an actual grape leaf onto thinly rolled out modelling paste, then cutting it out carefully. Let them dry with an appropriate bend to make them look natural. The tendrils are made of thinly rolled modelling paste, which you dry in the shape you eventually want them to be.

The wrapped pieces of cake are allowed to spill out of the cask.

No. 27. The Air Force Memorial.

NO. 27.   THE AIR FORCE MEMORIAL.

This cake was made for an air force wedding; of course the model was made to scale and covered with plastic icing, but it could also have been made in modelling paste or gum paste.

This monument is the one outside Pretoria commemorating the men and women in the South African Air Force who fell during the Second World War.

No. 28. The Voortrekker Monument.

NO. 28. THE VOORTREKKER MONUMENT.

This was a very difficult assignment. A very patriotic bride requested this as her wedding cake. To any South African the Voortrekker Monument is the very symbol of Afrikanerdom, and perhaps that was her reason for this singular request. My son built the model to scale, and I tried to make it as close to the original as was possible.

The nearest that I could however bring it to resemble a wedding cake was to have the figures of a bride and bridegroom on the steps replacing the figures of the mother and children on the actual monument. With a floral arrangement here and there I tried to soften the harsh lines without disturbing the monument image too much.

This was, in any case, an interesting and immense challenge, and the bride was happy, which is really the most important aspect of the whole thing.